FIGHTING ON MY KNEES

A Book of Prayers

Doris D. Harris

ISBN: 978-1-7327674-4-7
Library of Congress Control # 2018959962

Publishing in the USA by Vision to Fruition Publishing House
www.vision-fruition.com

Dedication

This book is dedicated to my dad Mott.

Oh, how proud You would be. You thought I could do anything.

You were always cheering me on. I love You and miss You more than words can truly express. This one's for You.

Forever Daddy's Girl
Love Dee

Topical Index

Preface

This book is for all those who believe in the power of prayer!

There is a war going on in the spirit causing things to manifest in the natural. The Bible tells us that the weapons we use to fight this spiritual battle are not natural weapons, but they are mighty through God and pull-down strongholds. Wow! That's good news. I have weapons in my arsenal that are mighty and powerful. And one of those weapons is Prayer.

Sometimes I can't physically do anything about a situation but pray. I can ask God to intervene, deliver, heal, save, or turn the situation around. I pray KNOWING God hears me and I wait in great expectation for the answers to MANIFEST!

This is how I fight for my husband, children, grandchildren, my marriage, my community, my neighborhood, and my friends! Down on my knees!

When people are asked to pray, many times their response is I don't know what to say. So, this book of prayers is intentionally written as a resource to use during Your prayer time.

So, after I've prayed, then what?

As I wait for the answers to manifest, with my mouth I DECLARE: to make known; a public notification of the TRUTH or EXISTENCE of something; the formal announcement of the beginning of a state or condition

I make an announcement and I make it known that what I prayed for I believe my petitions are answered. Why because I am praying according to the Will of God (which is His Word)

OUR WORDS HAVE POWER!

I speak it, declare it as it is.

IT IS FINISHED! IT IS HANDLED! IT IS DONE!

It's time to declare the answers manifested! So, I have included declarations with each prayer.

Wow! Aren't we thankful that God hears us and answers our prayers!

Prayer for Addiction

Mark 16:17 | Jude 1:9 | John 8:36

Father in the Name of Jesus,

I thank You that You came to set the captive free and who You set free is truly free.

You have delivered so many people before and I stand in faith and know that You are still a deliverer. I pray for _____. By the power and authority given to me in the name of Jesus Christ of Nazareth, I bind the spirit of addiction and I command addiction to come out of _____ right now in Jesus name! Addiction the Lord Jesus rebukes You back to the pit of hell and Your power is broken, annihilated and null and void in Jesus name! I pray every desire, appetite, urge, and craving is uprooted and dissolved, never to return. I pray _____ is filled with the Holy Spirit so he/she is empowered to resist temptation. Let _____ depend on You when hard days come and not seeking false comfort or happiness that comes from addiction.

I pray for accountability partners that are available to connect with him/her at any time day or night. Cause him/her to recognize the triggers and not fall back into old ways and habits. Let old things be passed away and all things become new in his/her life. Expose every false association sent by the enemy to cause him/her to fall. I pray _____ will have self-control and do what it takes to stay free not entangling himself/herself again with the yoke of bondage. I pray for complete restoration of peace, joy, and strength.

I pray he/she begins to fill up on the Word of God. Give him/her a hunger and a thirst for the word. Let his/her life forever be changed. Don't let him/her be ashamed to tell others how You delivered and set him/her free and I pray others will overcome by his/her testimony.

IN JESUS NAME, AMEN

Declaration

Father in the Name of Jesus,
Thank You for answering my Prayers!

I declare _____ is free from addiction! He/she is free, and all desires, appetites, urges, and cravings have been uprooted and dissolved! I declare _____ is filled with the holy ghost and is resisting temptation. He/she depends on You for peace, joy, and happiness does not seek false satisfaction from drugs, alcohol, food or any substance.

I declare all old things in his/her life are passed away and all things are new. He/she is strong in the Lord and in the power of Your might. He/she walks in self-control and is enjoying the peace of God which passes all understanding and the joy of the Lord is strengthening him/her day by day.

I declare _____ is an overcomer, delivered, transformed and free!

IT IS SO IN JESUS NAME

Prayer for Bullying

1 Samuel 1:6-7 | Psalm 140:1 | Psalm 7:1 | 2 Timothy 1:7 | Proverbs 20:22

Father in the Name of Jesus,

Thank You that in times like this we have a God we can call on who is well able to turn things around. So, father I pray for _____. I pray as Hannah prayed as she was bullied by Peninnah "look on Your servant's misery and remember me." Look on _____ who is being bullied, picked on, harassed and taunted and remember him/her/me. Bullying is dangerous, scary, stressful, unfair and mean so Lord rescue _____ from evil people and protect him/her/me from those who are violent. Don't let the bullying continue. I come to You for protection, save him/her/me from those who pursue him/her/me.

You did not give _____ a spirit of fear but love power and a sound mind. I pray that he/she/I will not be fearful or afraid any longer but with boldness will speak up, tell someone and ask for help. Make available a safe place where bullying can be exposed anonymously.

I plead the blood of Jesus over _____ and a hedge of protection around him/her/me and let there be no physical hurt or harm done.

Allow _____ to get help to work through what happened and learn how to move forward and get totally healed so this experience won't negatively impact his/her/my life. Please keep him/her/me from saying I will get even for this but help him/her/me to wait for You to handle it.

I pray for the bully(s) to be pricked in his/her/their heart(s) and convicted for being mean, give him/her/them a mind to stop. Father forgive the bully(s) for he/she/they know(s) not what he/she/they is/are doing and let Your goodness lead him/her/them to repentance. Draw him/her/them with loving kindness and show him/her/them mercy.

IN JESUS NAME, AMEN

Declaration

Father in the Name of Jesus,
Thank You for answering my Prayers!

I declare _____ is/am not being bullied!

I declare his/her/my mind is sound, clear and alert and not cluttered with what he/she/I went through!!

He/she/I is/am kept safe and no hurt or harm or danger will come nigh unto him/her/me! He/she/I is/am not looking back but pressing forward! I declare he/she/I is/am emotionally and mentally strong and there are no residual effects from the past and he/she/I do(es) not look like what he/she/I went through!

I declare _____ hold(s) no grudges but forgive(s) like Christ forgives.

And he/she/I is/am bold, strong, brave, loving, kind and victorious!

IT IS SO IN JESUS NAME

Prayer for Children

Jeremiah 29:11 | Proverbs 15:5

Father in the Name of Jesus,

I thank You that You love _____ and that Your promises in Your Word apply to him/her. I know that according to Jeremiah 29:11 that You know and have plans for_____. They are plans for good and not for disaster, to give him/her a future and a hope. I pray _____ is trained up in the way he/she should go, and he/she will not depart from it and with loving kindness draw him/her and let him/her confess that Jesus Christ is Lord.

I pray _____ will honor his/her father and mother so it may be well with him/her. I pray he/she is not foolish when he/she is disciplined but he/she is smart, receives and accepts correction and discipline with the right attitude learning and remembering that there are consequences for his/her actions. I bind the spirit of rebellion in the name of Jesus and lose the spirit of obedience to be manifested in his/her life. Let him/her reject any lying spirits and may he/she always be a truth teller.

As _____ grows up and learns to live life, I pray he/she listens to wise counsel and instructions, makes good choices and decisions and learns from his/her mistakes. I pray he/she connects with the right friends, and has the mind to say no when it is needed. Don't let _____ be a bully or be intentionally mean to others.

Let _____ know he/she was created in Your image and likeness and his/her true identity is according to the Word of God and not what someone else says. I pray he/she is not insecure and jealous of others but content and confident in the person You created him/her to be without second guessing his/her looks because of the world's standards. I pray _____ grows up to be a productive, law-abiding citizen in the community with a good work ethic, integrity, and moral values.

IN JESUS NAME, AMEN

Declaration

Father in the Name of Jesus,
Thank You for answering my Prayers!

I declare _____ is a born-again believer walking in the ways of God, living holy and doing what is right in the eyes of God. He/she honor's his/her mom and dad and is respectful to those in authority. I declare he/she is obedient, listens to instructions, has a good attitude when being corrected and disciplined, makes wise choices and decisions.

I declare _____ is a leader, not a follower, makes His own decisions and not afraid to say no. I declare _____ is who God created him/her to be and knows who he/she is in Christ and is not confused!

I declare _____ is nice, friendly, nonjudgmental and not a bully. He/she is strong, smart, handsome/beautiful, confident and blessed!

IT IS SO IN JESUS NAME

Prayer for Child - School

Colossians 3:23 | Proverbs 13:4

Father in the Name of Jesus,

I pray for _____ as he/she goes to school. I plead the blood of Jesus over him/her and a hedge of protection around him/her, safety on the way to school, via walking, on the bus or car. Send Your angelic angels to encamp round about the school, in the classrooms, hallways, playground, and restrooms and let those in attendance be safe.

Cause him/her to have a good attitude, be obedient and a mind to succeed. I pray _____ has everything he/she needs to be successful in learning. Let there be enough books, computers, and supplies needed for each day. I pray he/she is focused on learning and not distracted by the latest fashion, anything or anyone.

Let the classroom(s) have an atmosphere that is conducive for learning.

Proverbs 13:4 says lazy people want much but get little, but those who work hard will prosper.

I pray _____ will work with all his/her heart, in school as well as when doing homework and help him/her complete his/her assignments. I pray he/she is not lazy but has physical energy and mental stamina each day. I pray he/she gets enough rest at night and is energized every morning, excited to go to school. Place him/her in the right school with the right teacher. Show him/her favor with his/her teachers, students, and the staff.

I pray _____ understands the subjects he/she is being taught and the fearlessness to ask for help when needed. Give him/her good test-taking skills and let _____ see the fruit of his/her hard work and studying. I pray he/she is not a troublemaker or labeled as such and not pre-judged for any reason but given every opportunity to learn. Thank You for blessing the work of his/her hands.

IN JESUS NAME, AMEN

Declaration

Father in the Name of Jesus,
Thank You for answering my Prayers!

I declare today that _____ is safe, protected and covered with the blood of Jesus!

He/she is obedient, follows the rules and listens to instructions.

I declare he/she is learning, successful and God has supplied all his/her needs to be productive. The atmosphere is conducive for learning and there is no distractions. He/she is focused, driven, energized, works hard and gets his/her work done.

I declare _____ has favor with God, teachers, staff and students.

He/she knows hard work pays off and sees the fruit of his/her labor.

I declare _____is a good student, has a great attitude, is smart, excited to learn and a joy to have in class!

IT IS SO IN JESUS NAME

Prayer for Children's Friendships

Proverbs 13:20 | 1 Corinthians 15:33 | Proverbs 18:24

Father in the Name of Jesus,

I pray for _____ friendships. A true friend is valuable and not a relationship to take for granted. Your Word says walk with the wise and become wise, for a companion of fools suffers harm. I pray that You send wise friends into _____ life and remove and disconnect him/her from any relationships, connections, entanglements and false friends that are foolish and that are sent as a distraction from the enemy. Don't let _____ be misled: "bad company corrupts good character" and don't let _____ be one that misleads others down the wrong path. Lord, bless him/her with a mind to be himself/herself and not try to fit in and make friends with a certain "group" out of peer pressure or prejudge others by what someone else says.

There are "friends" who destroy each other, but a real friend sticks closer than a brother. I pray _____ and his/her friends will be real and honest with each other telling each other the truth even if it hurts and not backstabbers or fake. As iron sharpens iron, I pray his/her friendships are ones that bring encouragement, edification, and strength not jealousy or competition, so others can see what true friendship looks like.

I pray his/her friendships are healthy and not stressful or abusive in any way and that they will not lead him/her away from You. I pray he/she will know it's ok to have his/her own opinion with the boldness to speak up and know it's ok to agree to disagree. When they get angry with each other, I pray they work it out, learn how to solve the problem and forgive one another without holding a grudge. I pray they grow up together and have a long-lasting Godly friendship.

IN JESUS NAME, AMEN

Declaration

Father in the Name of Jesus,
Thank You for answering my Prayers!

I declare today that _____ has a great group of friends that are wise, smart, focused, making good choices and decisions.

All connections and entanglements with friends that were foolish, had wrong motives, desires and were sent as a distraction have been severed in Jesus name!

I declare _____ is not easily swayed and influenced and he/she is nonresponsive to peer pressure. _____ and his/her friends are real and honest with each other, they encourage, edify and strengthen each other and there is no competition or jealousy.

His/her friendship do not lead him/her away from You in any way.

IT IS SO IN JESUS NAME

Prayer for College Students

Proverbs 16:9 | Proverbs 16:3 | Phil 4:13

Father in the Name of Jesus,

Thank You for giving _____ the opportunity to further his/her/my education. I pray for overflowing resources to be readily available, so every financial need and obligation is met. I pray _____ will have books, computers, supplies and everything needed to be successful in college. Guide _____when he/she/I pick(s) a major so he/she/I will be in Your will and taking classes that are beneficial for his/her/my purpose knowing we make plans, but You Lord determine our steps.

I pray _____ will be disciplined, balancing his/her/my class attendance, homework and fun, making good use of his/her/my time. Help him/her/me learn good study habits and give him/her/me understanding, comprehension and memory of the information he/she/I learn(s), help when needed and good test taking skills. Let him/her/me see his/her/my studying is not in vain. Help _____ commit all his/her/my work to You so it will succeed.

Don't let _____ give up if he/she/I hit(s) a rough patch but give him/her/me the mind to pray and keep on going. Remind him/her/me You are with him/her/me and he/she/I can do all things through You because You give him/her/me the strength.

I bind every wicked plot and plan of the enemy that wants to steal kill and destroy, I declare it all to be canceled and shut down never to bring forth fruit in Jesus name! I pray he/she/I will not be easily influenced by others who are going down the wrong path and not focused. Help him/her/me to be steadfast, motivated, determined, focused, pure in thought and action living a life that exhibits true Christianity.

IN JESUS NAME, AMEN

Declaration

Father in the Name of Jesus,
Thank You for answering my Prayers!

I declare every financial obligation is met. He/she/I has/have books, computers and all supplies he/she/I need(s) to be successful. _____ is/am disciplined, goes/I go to class and makes good use of his/her/my time. He/she/I has/have good study habits with clear understanding, comprehension and memory of what he/she/I has/have studied and learned, and he/she/I know(s) his/her/my studying is not in vain. _____ will not give up!

I declare he/she/I is/am pure in thought, action, not easily influenced and live(s) a life that exhibits true Christianity.

I declare _____ is/am steadfast, focused, motivated, determined.

I declare _____ is/am a college graduate!

IT IS SO IN JESUS NAME

Prayer of Confession

Psalm 51:3-4 | Psalm 51:1-2 | 1 John 1:9

Father in the Name of Jesus,

Today I take full responsibility for my action's thoughts and motives. I know my transgressions, and my sin is always before me. I have messed up many times and it was against You, You only, I sinned and done what is evil in Your sight. So, I confess my sins. I confess every wrong thought desire motive and action. I confess saying yes to my own ways and desires and no to You and to what I knew was right to do.

Please forgive me when I crossed the line. Forgive me when I grieved the Holy Spirit. Forgive me for everything that I have done that is contrary to Your Word. Forgive me for everything that I have done even today that is not pleasing in Your sight. I'm sorry. Please have mercy on me and blot out my transgressions. Wash away all my iniquity and cleanse me from my sin. Forgive me for when I willingly did wrong. Forgive me if I caused someone else to stumble. Forgive me if my good was evil spoken of. I'm sorry for the times I did it my own way without seeking You first. Forgive me for the times the words of my mouth and the meditation of my heart was not acceptable to You. Forgive me for the times I gave in to temptation and didn't take the way of escape You made for me.

Father, I confess all my sins and I thank You that if I confess my sins Your Word says You are faithful and just to forgive me and cleanse me from all unrighteousness. Thank You for forgiving me and cleansing me. Thank You for Your mercy that holds back what I deserve and Your grace that gives me what I don't deserve.

I thank You for an opportunity to confess. I don't take it for granted. Give me a heart to quickly confess my sins and not get comfortable when I have done wrong. I just want to be pleasing in Your sight.

IN JESUS NAME, AMEN

Declaration

Father in the Name of Jesus,
Thank You for answering my Prayers!

When I confess God faithfully forgives me and so I live a life of confession! I am forgiven for my sins, sins of omission and commission, the things I said and done. I am cleansed from all unrighteousness and I stand in the righteousness of Christ.

I am free from guilt and shame and my past is not held against me. I forgive myself and I don't allow others to throw my mistakes up in my face. Sin is sin and I will confess them all! When I sin in Word thought or action I will confess!

I declare I am forgiven, cleansed and in right standing with God!

IT IS SO IN JESUS NAME.

Prayer for Court

John 7:24 | Proverbs 6:19 | Exodus 23:2

Father in the Name of Jesus,

I know we don't always get it right, so I thank You that You are a merciful and a forgiving God even though we don't deserve it. Please forgive _____ for whatever part he/she/I played in what he/she/I is/am being accused of. Help him/her/me to be truly remorseful and sorry and have a heart to make different choices, decisions, and actions. Show him/her/me mercy and grant him/her/me favor in court. Give him/her/me a fair chance and let it truly be said and applied in this case innocent until proven guilty. I pray that You place the right judge to preside over this case. One who will not pre-judge, judge unfairly, be bias, prejudice in any way and not judge by appearance but judge with righteous judgment. Bless him/her/me with the right lawyer, one that will truly represent him/her/me and his/her/my case even if he/she is court appointed.

Lord, You hate a false witness who pours out lies, so please let all witnesses be reliable so when they are called to testify in this dispute they are not swayed by the crowd to twist justice. In the name of Jesus, shut down and silence all lies, deception, false accusations, false testimony, and false blame and let the truth be told, heard, prevail and believed.

I pray that those who were impacted by what happened will forgive _____. Let him/her/me see what true mercy looks like and feels like and be pricked in his/her/my heart to change. I know that there are consequences for our actions, so I pray that the consequences will be in Your will for his/her/my life and not the consequences made by emotions, quotas that need to be met or to make him/her/me an example for others to learn from.

IN JESUS NAME, AMEN

Declaration

Father in the Name of Jesus,
Thank You for answering my Prayers!

I declare today that _____ has/have been forgiven for his/her/my wrong. I declare _____ is/am shown mercy, favor and is given a fair chance. I declare the right judge is presiding over the case. I declare no prejudgment, bias or prejudice will prevail. I declare the right lawyer and representation has been given.

I declare all false testimonies, lies, deception, false blame and false accusations have been destroyed and annihilated at the root and justice is not twisted! I declare truth is told, heard, believed and it prevails! Forgiveness is abounding and mercy overflowing!

I declare mercy, fair consequences and lessons learned.

IT IS SO IN JESUS NAME

Daily Prayer

Philippians 4:8 | 1 Peter 5:8

Father in the Name of Jesus,

I thank You for waking me up to experience another day. Forgive me of my sins. Cleanse me from all unrighteousness. I plead the blood of Jesus and a hedge of protection around me and my family today.

Thank You, that I rise empowered, victorious, strong, and courageous. Let my discernment be keen and my mind focused. Today I walk in power and authority and in the name of Jesus I bind every wicked plot, plan, and scheme of the enemy that wants to frustrate my day and I lose the peace of God, order and perfect harmony in Jesus name!

I will not worry about anything, instead, I will pray about everything with thanksgiving, so I will experience the peace of God. My mind is alert and sober and I am not overwhelmed by problems and the cares of this world. Thank You for giving me Your Word so I am not ignorant of Satan's devices and to use against principalities, powers, rulers of the darkness of this world and spiritual wickedness in high places.

Father lead me by Your spirit today, so I won't fulfill the lust of the flesh. Help me to think before I speak and cause my emotions to be stable, so I am not moved by others actions. Help me to exhibit self-control in every area and the fruit of the spirit be manifested in my life. Help me to be a good steward over my time and a light so someone may say Your God will be my God.

I pray that I make intentional moves today even if that is resting and not wasting the day on unproductive busyness.

No weapon formed against me, my family, my finances, my health, my mind, my ministry, my _____, my _____, or my _____ shall prosper!

IN JESUS NAME, AMEN

Declaration

Father in the Name of Jesus,
Thank You for answering my Prayers!

I declare today I walk in power and authority and the enemies plans against me today have been disrupted, canceled, thwarted and bound in Jesus name! I have peace and things are in order and working in perfect harmony!

I have the Word of God in my arsenal to use against the enemy and I am not ignorant of His devices! The Holy Spirit is leading me, my emotions are stable, and I am walking in self-control! My family and I are covered with the blood of Jesus and a hedge of protection is around us.

I am empowered victorious, strong and courageous! My discernment is keen, and my mind is focused.

IT IS SO IN JESUS NAME

Prayer for Depression

Psalm 42:11 | Philippians 4:8

Father in the Name of Jesus,

I pray for _____.

I bind the spirit of depression in the name of Jesus and I loose the joy of the Lord to be made manifest and to strengthen _____. I bind the spirit of heaviness in the name of Jesus and I loose the spirit of praise.

I pray _____ will make a conscious decision to stop and say as David said "why am I discouraged? Why is my heart so sad? I will put my hope in God, I will praise him again! Give _____ the strength to praise You in spite of how he/she/I feel(s).

When _____ begin(s) to feel downcast or sad, give him/her/ me the mind and the strength to fight to know the weapons we use are mighty and pull-down strongholds. Give him/her/me a mind to flush out the negative lies from the enemy with the Word of God each and every day.

Keep _____ from becoming a prisoner to negative thoughts. I declare _____ has/have the mind of Christ so cause him/her/me to be nonresponsive to depression and suicidal thoughts. Help him/her/me to think about whatever is true, noble, right, pure, lovely, admirable and things that are excellent or praiseworthy.

Don't let him/her/me struggle silently and alone. Give _____ a person to call who will be there to help and not judge. Don't let _____ give up! I pray he/she/I will walk in liberty and wisdom and get professional help without the fear or stigma of being judged if needed.

Render the enemy powerless and ineffective. Bring His plans to naught.

Help _____ to keep his/her/my mind stayed on You so he/she/I will experience perfect peace. I thank You for a renewed mind.

IN JESUS NAME, AMEN

Declaration

Father in the Name of Jesus,
Thank You for answering my Prayers!

I declare _____ is/am free from depression, emotionally strong and experiencing the joy of the Lord! He/she/I will bless the Lord at all times and His praises are in _____ mouth.

I declare _____ is/am thinking only about what is true, noble, right, pure, lovely, admirable and praiseworthy! _____ take(s) all negative thoughts captive and makes them obey Christ. All assignments from the enemy against _____ mind have been bound and cancelled! I declare liberty and freedom!
I declare _____ has/have the mind of Christ, is/am nonresponsive to depression and his/her/my mind has been renewed!

IT IS SO IN JESUS NAME

Prayer for Finances

Philippians 4:19 | Proverbs 3:9 | 2 Corinthians 9:7 |
2 Corinthians 9:10

Father in the Name of Jesus,

I thank You that You are Jehovah Jireh our provider. Thank You for _____ having money to be able to pay his/her/my bills, buy food and do the things needed financially to live because You God supply all his/her/my needs according to Your riches in glory.

I ask You to forgive _____ for all the times he/she/I wasn't a good steward over what You blessed him/her/me with financially, the times he/she/I was lazy, stingy and wouldn't help the poor. Help him/her/me to be more responsible by learning the fundamental principles of prosperity so that he/she/I will not continually be defeated, lacking, struggling or living paycheck to paycheck.

My prayer is that he/she/I will not love this world or the things it offers and that he/she/I won't lust in the flesh or eyes for things that he/she/I cannot afford to buy.

I pray that he/she/I will honor You with his/her/my substance and with the first fruits of all increase. I pray that his/her/my giving is done cheerfully and not out of pressure or to be seen and as he/she/I give(s), I pray You provide and increase his/her/my resources and rebuke the devourer.

I bind the spirit of poverty and I pray all its works and fruit of debt, lack, scarcity, shortage, deficiency, poorness, laziness, begging and borrowing be uprooted and dissolved in the name of Jesus and I loose financial increase, overflow, plenty and sustainability.

Thank You that his/her/my giving and being a good steward over his/her/my finances is not in vain.

IN JESUS NAME, AMEN

Declaration

Father in the Name of Jesus,
Thank You for answering my Prayers!

I declare today _____ has/have more than enough to pay bills, buy food and do what is needed to live! He/she/I is/am financially responsible and a good steward over all finances. I declare that _____ has/have self-control and honors God with the first fruits of all increase and substance.

I declare no weapon formed against his/her/my finances will prosper and _____ is/am free from debt, shortage, deficiency, poorness, begging and borrowing. Every seed that _____ has/have sown is producing a financial harvest and I declare financial increase, overflow, plenty and abundance is his/hers/mine.

IT IS SO IN JESUS NAME

Prayer for Forgiveness

Colossians 3:13 | Matthew 6:12 | Matthew 18:22 | Luke 23:34

Father in the Name of Jesus,

Your Word says make allowances for each other's faults and forgive anyone who offends You. Remember, the Lord forgave You, so You must forgive others. So, Lord, I thank You that You are a forgiving and a merciful God. You looked beyond our faults and seen our need. Your Word is very clear that we must forgive even seventy times seven In one day. Lord, forgiving someone who did us wrong can be hard sometimes, so please give _____ a mind to say as You said Father forgive them for, they know not what they do.

Lord, he/she/I want(s) to be a doer of Your Word and not just a hearer so help _____ to truly forgive who did him/her/me wrong and to show unconditional love. Lord, take out the stony heart and give him/her/me a heart of flesh. Wash his/her/my mind, wash his/her/my attitude with the water of the word. Help him/her/me be kind and compassionate, forgiving as You forgave him/her/me. Don't let bitterness, envy, resentment or the spirit of offense take root in his/her/my heart. I bind the spirit of unforgiveness and loose the grace of God. Take away any pain, anger and hurt that comes from the memory of what happened and cause the fruit of patience and love to abound.

Whatever part he/she/I played in the situation, please forgive him/her/me and don't let him/her/me be too proud to say I'm sorry, knowing it's not a sign of weakness but strength. Being strong enough to do what it takes to become more like You and not let his/her/my flesh rule and reign.

Please forgive him/her/me as he/she/I forgive(s) others and I pray he/she/they will see the love of Christ in action.

IN JESUS NAME, AMEN

Declaration

Father in the Name of Jesus,

Thank You for answering my Prayers!

I declare _____ show(s) unconditional love, compassion, forgiveness and kindness. _____ is/am free from all bitterness, envy, resentment, offense and unforgiveness.

I declare that _____ extend(s) only patience, love and grace and he/she/I show(s) the love of God in action. _____ is/am not too proud to say sorry. _____is/am a light for others to see and his/her/my good is not evil spoken of.

I declare _____ is/am strong, loving, patient, merciful and forgiving.

IT IS SO IN JESUS NAME

Prayer for Government

1 Timothy 2:1-2 | Proverbs 3:21 | Proverbs 75:7

Father in the Name of Jesus,

I pray and intercede with thanksgiving for all those in high positions, that we may lead a peaceful and quiet life, Godly and dignified in every way.

Lord, I lift the government in the city of _____ and the state of_____. I pray that You put Christian leaders in office that will yield to the Holy Spirit and allow You to guide their decision making and cause Your will to be done. I pray that they are men and women who will govern with a moral compass and integrity.

I pray they have a heart for all people and a true interest in what is needed in the communities. Open their eyes to the real problems affecting the city and reveal what is lacking and what is needed to bring change, school improvement, jobs, better healthcare and an increase in wages. Give them wisdom, common sense, and discernment when handling difficult decisions, making policies and passing laws. During meetings keep them focused, their minds clear and let them be peacemakers.

Since You God are the judge and You put down one and set up another I pray You expose and remove any in office who are involved in deceit, hidden agendas, corruption, financial wrongdoing, manipulation, and embezzlement.

Lord, bless their families. I pray they are faithful to their spouses, he/she lives a Godly life and the men are good providers.

Remember our law enforcement workers who put their lives on the line daily. Guide them and protect them as they keep the city safe. Give them wisdom, strength, courage, compassion, and keen discernment while on duty.

IN JESUS NAME, AMEN

Declaration

Father in the Name of Jesus,
Thank You for answering my Prayers!

I declare the government in the city of _____ and the state of_____ are ran by Christian leaders who yield to the Holy Spirit. I declare the will of the Lord is done. They are men and women who govern with a moral compass and integrity.

I declare they have a heart for all people's needs, and they are making decisions that cause change, school improvement, increased job rates, better health care and an increase in wages.

Our law enforcement is covered with the blood of Jesus and kept safe. They are guided by the Holy Spirit, they have wisdom, strength, courage, compassion and keen discernment while on duty.

IT IS SO IN JESUS NAME

Prayer for Healing

Acts 10:38 | Matthew 9:35 | Luke 13:12 | 3 John 1:2 |
Acts 9:34

Father in the Name of Jesus,

I thank You that You are Jehovah-Rapha the God who heals.

I lift _____ up before You. The enemy has oppressed him/her/me with the spirit of infirmity. Your Word says You healed all that were oppressed of the devil. I know Your track record! You healed every disease and sickness and I know that You are the same God.

By the power and authority given to me in the name of Jesus, the spirit of infirmity I bind you and command you to go iu the name of Jesus! Infirmity the Lord Jesus rebukes You back to hell and any fruits, residue or roots be dried up, uprooted and dissolved in the name of Jesus!

I loose resurrection life, health, healing and wholeness in Jesus name.

I pray _____ will prosper and be in health, even as his/her/my soul prospers. I plead the blood of Jesus over _____body from the top of his/her/my head to the souls of his/her/my feet. I pray for complete restoration and wholeness over all organs, veins, muscles, cells, glands, tissue and blood vessels and that they return to their healthy state and function normally.

I pray there are no adverse side effects from medications, supplements and or medical treatments in the name of Jesus.

Replenish his/her/my physical energy and strength. And where there is mental and emotional fatigue I pray for peace and rest. I thank You for his/her/my complete deliverance and healing.

Jesus Christ heals You, get up!

IN JESUS NAME, AMEN

Declaration

Father in the Name of Jesus,
Thank You for answering my Prayers!

I declare today that _____ is/am healed and free from all sickness and disease! _____ is/am prosperous and in good health living to declare the works of the Lord

I declare _____ is/am covered with the blood of Jesus and all organs, veins, muscles, cells, glands, tissue and blood vessels are restored, healthy and function normally. He/she/I is/am free from all side effects from medication. _____ is mentally and emotionally strong with physical energy, stamina, and strength.

I declare _____ is/am strong, healed, healthy and made whole!

IT IS SO IN JESUS NAME

Prayer for Homeless

Psalm 40:1-2 | Proverbs 19:17 | Matthew 25:40

Father in the Name of Jesus,

I know people become homeless for a variety of reasons, so I pray we don't judge them, being mindful of the fact it could be us.

I pray for those who are homeless today asking You to remember them, and as they wait patiently for You to help, turn to them, hear their cry and lift them out of the pit of despair. Cause them to have hope in the midst of this difficult journey. I pray You give them a warm place to sleep tonight, a place to shield them from the elements during the day and keep them safe. Cover them with the blood of Jesus.

Bless them with food to sustain them and access to basic needs such as personal hygiene items. I pray You connect them with compassionate, concerned people, agencies and workers that will help them obtain and retain affordable housing. Provide them with the necessary resources that will help them resolve this crisis and empower them to become self-sufficient. Give them the help they need to make a lasting change, build their confidence and restore their dignity.

Keep children together with their families and don't let them be separated. Remember the teenagers on the street. I pray that they receive support services that will help them learn life management skills, budgeting and move towards independence.

Let the homeless feel and see the love of Jesus in action. Give them the strength and willpower to keep going to rebuild their lives.

Don't let us forget about those in need remembering if we/I help the poor we/I lend to the Lord. Give us a mind to help others remembering when we do, we do it unto You.

IN JESUS NAME, AMEN

Declaration

Father in the Name of Jesus,
Thank You for answering my Prayers!

I declare today that the homeless are not forgotten by God and His ears are open to their cry! They have a safe place to shield them from the elements and tonight they will have a warm bed to sleep in. They are covered with the blood of Jesus and a hedge of protection is around them.

They will receive housing, resources, food, and personal hygiene items. They have a sound mind; peace and all confidence and dignity has been restored.

I declare today they will be shown concern, compassion, grace, mercy and the love of Jesus in action.

IT IS SO IN JESUS NAME

Prayer for Husband

Acts 13:22 | Luke 10:27 | Proverbs 3:5-6 |Romans 12:2 | Ephesians 5:25

Father in the Name of Jesus,

I pray _____ is a man after Your own heart that loves You with all His heart, soul, strength and mind. I pray He walks in power and authority fully aware of who He is in Christ. Let him trust in You with all His heart and does not depend on His own understanding but acknowledges You so You can direct His path as He leads his/our family. I pray He is not conformed to this world, but He is transformed and changed by renewing His mind in Your Word day by day. Bless him to be wise and keep him faithful to his/our covenant. I pray that He loves _____ as Christ loves the church and You are first in His life. Let him declare as for me and my house, we will serve the Lord. Give him a hunger for Your Word with good study habits and a prayer life.

Don't let him be lazy and unproductive but cause him to be diligent with a good work ethic, be a good provider and a good steward over what You blessed him with. I pray He is reliable and trustworthy. Let His yes be yes and His no be no. Don't let him hold a grudge when they/we argue but let him be quick to forgive. Disconnect him from those who are a bad influence and foolish and connect him with friends that have a pure heart, integrity, and wisdom. Let His discernment be sharp making him aware of wolves in sheep's clothing. Keep a hedge of protection around him and show him favor in the marketplace. I pray He is healed from any past hurts and wounds that would try to hold him hostage. Let him be whole and free.

(If He has children): let him be a good father who is present and consistent in their lives, spending quality time listening, talking, playing, guiding, disciplining, encouraging, affirming and validating them, praying with and for them, loving them in action and teaching His son(s) how to become a man/men.

IN JESUS NAME, AMEN

Declaration

Father in the Name of Jesus,
Thank You for answering my Prayers!

I declare that _____ is a man after God's own heart. He walks in power and authority and knows who He is in Christ. I declare He is wise, faithful, and a keeper of His covenant. I declare _____ is a dependable worker, a good provider and a good steward over His finances and time. He is reliable, trustworthy and there is a hedge of protection is around him and He has favor in the marketplace. He is whole and healed from all past hurts and wounds.

I declare He is a good father who builds his children up and not tears them down. He is a good listener who gives wise advice. He is training them up in the way they should go and providing for their needs.

IT IS SO IN JESUS NAME.

Prayer for Marriage

1 Corinthians 7:5 | 1 Corinthians 13:4-5

Father in the Name of Jesus,

I thank You for the covenant of marriage. I pray _____
will love _____ as Christ loves the church and she/I will
submit to him as her/my husband. I pray they/we will love each
other unconditionally on good days, and bad, in Word and action.

Let there be unity in their/our home and a made-up mind to stay
till death do they/us part and divorce not being an option. Teach
them/us how to handle conflict and disagreements and how to
resolve arguments and issues without crossing the line. I pray
they/we will show each other grace when one makes a mistake
and not go to bed angry and upset. Let both of them/us have a
heart to easily say I'm sorry and to do what it takes to keep the
marriage strong, united, fun and exciting. Let them/us always be
mindful of why they/we fell in love. I pray they/we don't
deprive each other, making any room for temptation from the
enemy. Bless their/our coming together with love, passion, and
satisfaction. Break and dissolve any ungodly soul ties and
disconnect and sever any friendships or relationships devised
by the enemy to steal, kill and destroy the marriage.

I pray that they/we will work together financially making
choices and doing what's best for their/our household. Help
them/us to communicate effectively not leaving room for the

enemy to cause confusion and division. Let them/us truly show love in action by being patient, kind, not easily angered and not keeping records of wrong. Let them/us walk together as one not allowing others to penetrate through the unity causing separation. Don't let them/us embarrass each other in public but show only respect.

Lord be the head of their/our marriage, rule and reign.

IN JESUS NAME, AMEN

Declaration

Father in the Name of Jesus,
Thank You for answering my Prayers!

I declare _____ marriage is blessed! They/we are walking together in agreement and united as one. Their/our marriage is filled with grace making allowances for our faults.

They/we communicate effectively, and divorce is not a part of their/our vocabulary.
I declare they/we are patient, kind, not easily angered, don't keep records of wrong and showing love in action.

I declare _____ marriage is strong, fun, exciting, passionate, united and blessed.

IT IS SO IN JESUS NAME

Prayer for Neighborhood

Galatians 5:14 | Matthew 5:14

Father in the Name of Jesus,

I thank You for _____ neighborhood. Your Word says love Your neighbor as Yourself. I pray that he/she/I will do this by showing the love of Christ in action and being a light. I pray the entire neighborhood will be born again, a city on a hill that cannot be hidden. Place the right people in his/her/my neighborhood who are friendly, hospitable and have a desire for peace and safety who will look out for one another. I pray the neighborhood is a safe place where children can go outside and play without fear of violence or being hurt.

I pray all neighbors collectively are attentive and alert to what's going on around them/us and aware when something is off and not right. Expose any hidden agenda of the enemy that wants to infiltrate the neighborhood with drugs, crime, violence, illegal activity or gangs so that they/we are not ignorant of Satan's plan, so they/we can pray effectively. Shut it down and bring it to naught in the name of Jesus.

I pray they/we will build healthy relationships with each other and find common ground even in their/our differences. Lord, help them/us to promote respect for diversity and different cultures making all residents feel welcome.

Let there be peace and safety up and down each street and in each home. If there is any abuse make it stop, bring conviction, repentance and let the love of God manifest and prevail. Where there is discord or conflict, bring harmony and peace.

IN JESUS NAME, AMEN

Declaration

Father in the Name of Jesus,
Thank You for answering my Prayers!

I declare _____ neighborhood is a peaceful safe place. The neighbors are nice, friendly, hospitable, attentive and alert. I declare the blood of Jesus covers each home and no harm comes nigh to their/our dwelling places. The children can play outside safely and there is no drugs, crime, violence or gang activity.

The relationship between the neighbors is healthy, fosters respect, trust and all prejudices have been bound and evicted and unity prevails! Each home is filled with the peace of God and any and all abuse has been exposed, stopped and the love of Christ prevails!

I declare the love of God is spread throughout the community and His peace is manifested!

IT IS SO IN JESUS NAME

Prayer for Night Time

Ecclesiastes 5:3 | Psalm 3:24 | Psalm 91:11

Father in the Name of Jesus,

I love You so much Lord and I thank You for _____ having the opportunity to enjoy another day. Even through rough patches and challenges You faithfully carry him/her/me through from day to day. Thank You.

Thank You for protection and watching over him/her/me. I know we do things and say things sometimes that cross the line so please forgive him/her/me for any and all sins today.

Help _____ to give all his/her/my cares and concerns to You tonight because too many worries leads to nightmares.

When _____ lay(s) down tonight I pray he/she/I will not be afraid and his/her/my sleep will be sweet. He/she/I will not toss or turn from anxiety or worry from today's event's or for what may or may not happen tomorrow. He/she/I will sleep peacefully, get a good night's rest and relaxation for his/her/my mind and body. Lord, replenish his/her/my energy, stamina and strength for tomorrow.

Help _____ to exhibit self-control and make good use of his/her/my time even at night knowing it is useless to work so hard from early morning until late at night, anxiously working for food to eat because it is Your desire that we rest.

I plead the blood of Jesus over the windows and doorpost of his/her/my home and ask You, Lord, to send Your angels to encamp round about the property. Watch over him/her/me and his/her/my family tonight and keep them/us safe.

Thank You for Your faithfulness and a place to lay down tonight. I pray he/she/I will make even better choices tomorrow and draw even closer to You.

IN JESUS NAME, AMEN

Declaration

Father in the Name of Jesus,
Thank You for answering my Prayers!

I declare tonight _____ will lie down concern-free, worry-free, carefree, not afraid and his/her/my sleep will be sweet. He/she/I will not toss and turn but will sleep peacefully, get a good night's rest and relaxation for his/her/my mind and body.

I declare _____ will wake up physically and mentally refreshed and replenished, and with energy, stamina, and strength.

I declare the blood of Jesus covers the doorpost of his/her/my home and angels have been dispatched to protect and guard _____ and his/her/my family.

I declare peace, rest, protection, safety, good dreams, and an anxiety free, stress-free, worry-free night!

IT IS SO IN JESUS NAME

Prayer for Pastors

Jeremiah 3:15 |1 Corinthian 2:4 | John 21:17

Father in the Name of Jesus,

I lift pastor _____ up before You. I pray he/she is filled with the Holy Spirit with the evidence of speaking in other tongues as the spirit gives utterance. I pray he/she gives himself/herself continually to prayer and to the ministry of the word. I pray he/she is a shepherd after Your own heart who guides with knowledge and understanding and studies to show himself/herself approved. Give him/her revelation and knowledge of Your word, insight and keen discernment. Let his/her teaching and preaching not be with wise and persuasive words, but with a demonstration of Your power and sound doctrine as he/she feeds Your sheep. Give him/her wisdom and courage to make the hard decisions as he/she is led by Your spirit and don't let him/her be bound by tradition, habits or a program but let him/her be so intuned with You that You will have free reign. Let everything he/she does be done as unto You and not for fame, fortune, status or glory.

I pray he/she is faithful to You, the church and to his/her spouse. Don't let his/her good be evil spoken of. Give him/her wisdom to physically rest from week to week and the boldness to say no when needed. Bless his/her finances and let every need be met. Give him/her accountability partners, co-laborers who he/she can be accountable to, men and women who will hold him/her up as Aaron and Hur held up Moses' arms during battle. Give him/her good faithful helpers in the ministry, those he/she can be confident in relinquishing duties to who will get the job done. Let him/her know he/she is not alone. Don't let him/her get weary in well doing and let grace be multiplied unto him/her for this assignment.

IN JESUS NAME, AMEN

Declaration

Father in the Name of Jesus,
Thank You for answering my Prayers!

I declare _____ is called and chosen by God, filled with the holy ghost and a man/woman after Gods' heart. He/she has a burden for souls and is constant in prayer. He/she guides with knowledge and understanding and studies to show himself/herself approved. He/she has keen discernment, insight and teaches and preaches with a demonstration of Gods power.

I declare _____ is free from tradition and is in tune and lead by the Holy Spirit. His/her finances are blessed, and all needs are met. He/she has faithful co-laborers and is not alone.

I declare _____ is blessed, faithful, focused, prayerful, anointed and graced for this assignment.

IT IS SO IN JESUS NAME

Prayer for Prisoners

Acts 12:5 | Ecclesiastes 7:9

Father in the Name of Jesus,

As the church prayed earnestly for Peter while He was in prison, I pray for _____. I pray he/she has an encounter with You and comes to the truth, knowledge and confesses that Jesus Christ is Lord and is born again so he/she will experience true freedom that's only found in You. I pray he/she will experience Your forgiveness and have a genuine remorse for the things he/she has done. I pray that _____ will not continue to repeat this behavior and bad decision making but will learn from his/her mistakes and truly repent and change. Help him/her to control his/her temper being fully mindful of the consequences for his/her actions. Help him/her to make wise choices and avoid corrupt friendships in prison that will lead to more trouble.

Give him/her a mind to respect the prison staff and keep him/her safe from assault and violence. I pray he/she takes advantage of the classes and programs that are offered inside knowing this will benefit him/her when reentering society. I pray he/she has the right cellmate and that they get along, both having a mindset to make changes and learn from their mistakes. When he/she is released, let all resources needed to become a productive member of society, be available to him/her and that he/she does what it takes to stay out of trouble never to return to prison (jail) again. Show him/her favor as he/she looks for jobs and applies for housing. Give him/her friends that will be a positive influence in his/her life and disconnect him/her from the old friends that he/she doesn't need to hang around with.

Don't let him/her be forgotten and tossed aside by his/her family and friends. Let them show love and compassion remembering we have all made mistakes.

IN JESUS NAME, AMEN

Declaration

Father in the Name of Jesus,
Thank You for answering my Prayers!

I declare _____ is a born-again believer and free in Christ, _____ has learned from his/her mistakes and is in control of his/her temper. He/she is making wise decisions, staying out of trouble and avoiding corrupt friendships. _____ and his/her cellmate have been strategically placed together by God and it's all working together for good.

He/she respects all staff and is kept safe from all assault and violence. I plead the blood of Jesus over _____ and over the doorpost of the cell. He/she is remorseful, has learned from past mistakes and his/her past is not held against him/her.

I declare _____ is remembered, loved, supported, reformed and free!

IT IS SO IN JESUS NAME

Prayer for Salvation

John 3:16 | 2 Peter 3:9 | John 6:44 |Jeremiah 31:3 |
Mark 4:8 | Acts 2:37

Father in the Name of Jesus,

I thank You that You so loved the world that You gave Your one and only son, that whosoever believes in him shall not perish but have eternal life.

I thank You that You are patient, not wanting anyone to perish, but everyone to come to repentance. So today I pray for _____ that he/she will come to understand that he/she is a sinner and there is a price for sin and You paid that price for him/her.

I pray he/she will not continue to be comfortable in sin. Cause him/her to feel empty and unsatisfied without You. Snatch him/her out of darkness and cause _____ to know and experience the grace of God. Father draw him/her to You. Draw him/her with Your loving kindness. I pray _____ hears the good news and is pricked in his/her heart causing him/her to cry out what must I do to be saved. Let him/her come to the truth and knowledge and confess that Jesus Christ is Lord. Save him/her before it's too late. Fill _____ with the Holy Spirit with the evidence of speaking in other tongues, that produces the fruit of the spirit and empowers him/her to live a holy and sanctified life.

Let the seed of the Word fall on good soil and take root in his/her heart causing him/her to be like a tree planted by streams of water, bearing fruit each season.

I pray he/she will be totally surrendered to You and that You will rule and reign in his/her life. I pray he/she will not look back but will forever press towards the mark continually cultivating his/her relationship with You. I pray he/she will learn the Word of God and apply it, being a doer of the Word and not a hearer only, continually being transformed by renewing his/her mind. Let his/her light shine and may he/she be a witness, sharing the gospel, making disciples so someone else may say, what must I do to be saved.

IN JESUS NAME, AMEN

Declaration

Father in the Name of Jesus,
Thank You for answering my Prayers!

I declare _____ is a whosoever, born-again Christian! Old things are passed away and all things have become new in his/her life. He/she is filled with the Holy Spirit with the evidence of speaking in other tongues and empowered to resist the enemy.

He/she is pressing towards the mark and not looking back. He/she is an overcomer walking in victory, more than a conqueror and can do all things through Christ. He/she will not backslide but will continually draw nigh unto God.

I declare _____ is strong, bold, walking in power, transformed, saved, born again and the temple of the Holy Spirit.

IT IS SO IN JESUS NAME

Prayer for Schools

Proverbs 4:13 | Proverbs 15:13 | Proverbs 28:21

Father in the name of Jesus

Your Word says to hold onto instruction do not let it go; guard it well for it is Your life. Lord, I know that many wish they could go to school to learn and can't, so I thank You for our educational system in _____ and the opportunity to learn. Thank You for the teachers, teacher's aid's, principals, administrators, secretaries, office staff, security, cafeteria workers, janitors, librarians, counselors, nurses, coaches and all those who work at _____. I pray they will welcome the students and each other daily with a cheerful heart and a smiling face and let Your peace permeate the atmosphere.

I pray the school board and all the decision makers will work together with a cohesive mindset focused on providing quality leadership and education regardless of economic status or ethnicity not showing any partiality. Let them hire the right teachers and staff that have a heart for students. Let them recognize what is effective and what isn't and make the necessary changes needed to improve any areas that are experiencing lack.

Let there be enough funding available to meet the needs of the school and to pay teachers and staff appropriately. Let there be no lack but let the resources that are needed be readily available. I pray for good healthy lunches and after-school activities.

I pray there is a secure safe place at _____ for students to secretly expose bullies, as well as safety precautions and practices in place in case of an emergency to keep students and staff safe.

I plead the blood of Jesus and a hedge of protection around _____. Send Your angels to encamp round about the building and in the halls. Keep everyone safe today.

IN JESUS NAME, AMEN

Declaration

Father in the Name of Jesus,
Thank You for answering my Prayers!

I declare that _____ is a great school, a safe place, covered with the blood of Jesus and a hedge of protection is all around. All needs are met, there is no lack or shortage of funds and resources. They provide good healthy lunches and productive after-school activities.

I declare all bullies are exposed, silenced, shut down and reformed.

They provide quality leadership and a good education. All teachers and staff have a heart for the students and a drive to help them be successful.

I declare _____ is providing quality education, has an excellent group of teachers and staff and the students are being educated.

IT IS SO IN JESUS NAME

Prayer for Singles

1 Corinthians 7:32 | Ephesians 6:10-11 | Proverbs 4:23 |
1 Timothy 4:12

Father in the name of Jesus

I thank You for _____. Thank You for his/her/my time of singleness. I pray he/she/I won't let his/her/my singleness be like a negative label placed on him/her/me. Help _____to see it's not a curse but a blessing to have more time to focus on doing the Lord's work, sitting at Your feet, praying, fasting, learning Your ways, pleasing You, growing in the things of God and cultivating the relationship.

Help him/her/me to be strong in the Lord and in Your mighty power and put on the whole armor of God so he/she/I can stand against the schemes and tricks of the enemy. I thank You that the Holy Spirit empowers him/her/me to resist the enemy. I pray he/she/I will honor You with his/her/my mind and body while remembering that he's/she's/ I'm the temple of the Holy Spirit.

When loneliness pops up, please manifest Your presence and bring contentment and comfort. Keep him/her/me from falling and giving into temptation, and fleshly urges.

I pray _____ is/am a Godly example for others in speech, life, love, faith and purity. Guard him/her/my heart against ungodly influences and distractions sent by the enemy. Help him/her/me to focus on becoming more like You and doing what You called him/her/me to do.

You have work for him/her/me to do and if You have a spouse for him/her/me then great and if You don't great. Please don't let him/her/me be so consumed with the thought and idea of marriage that he/she/I can't even enjoy life today while single.

Satisfy him/her/me completely and totally so he/she/I will not seek happiness and satisfaction from others. I pray he/she/I will delight himself/herself/myself in You.

IN JESUS NAME, AMEN

Declaration

Father in the Name of Jesus,
Thank You for answering my Prayers!

I declare _____ is/am successfully single! His/her/my time of singleness is a blessing from God. _____ is/am strong, confident and not comparing his/her/my life to others. He/she/I is/am not lonely but content and satisfied in Jesus.

I declare _____ is/am healed from all past hurts, wounds and breakups and is whole in Jesus name. He/she/I know(s) who he/she/I is/am and confident that he/she/I was created for greatness! _____ is/am living his/her/my best life and focused on God!

I declare _____ is/am strong, bold, confident, focused, celibate, chaste, whole, happy, walking in purpose and full of joy!

IT IS SO IN JESUS NAME

Prayer for Single Parents

Psalm 127:3 | Proverbs 3:6 | Ephesians 6:4

Father in the Name of Jesus,

I thank You that _____ has/have the awesome opportunity to be a parent. I pray as a single parent, he/she/I will not feel less valued than those who have 2 parents in the home. Thank You that You have blessed him/her/me with children because children are a gift and a reward from You.

I pray he/she/I will be a parent who prays continually not just in an emergency. Remind him/her/me that You will never leave him/her/me, and You are a very present help at all times. Give him/her/me wisdom. He/she/I can't do this without You Lord so in all his/her/my ways I pray he/she/I will acknowledge You, so You can guide and direct his/her/my path.

Help him/her/me not to provoke his/her/my children to anger but bring them up with discipline and instruction from the Lord. Help him/her/me to do the best he/she/I can without compromising Godly values. I pray he/she/I will be a Godly example in their/my home, not double-minded and unstable. I pray he/she/I will learn from mistakes and get healed from any old or childhood issues, so they don't negatively impact his/her/my child(ren).

Give him/her/me the liberty and a safe place he/she/I can turn to when feeling overwhelmed, needing a listing ear or help. I pray for friends and family who will willingly babysit so he/she/I can get a break, some alone time and adult time.

Lord, it's not always easy to provide for the family with one income so I pray for financial increase. I pray that he/she/I will be responsible with what You blessed him/her/me with and let every need be met, bills paid, food on the table, school clothes and basic necessities provided. Thank You that have graced him/her/me to be a parent.

IN JESUS NAME, AMEN

Declaration

Father in the Name of Jesus,
Thank You for answering my Prayers!

I declare _____ is a great single parent! God is with him/her/me leading, guiding and directing his/her/my steps and his/her/my home is filled with love, joy and the peace of God.

I declare _____ is/am a Godly example in his/her/my home, does not compromise and his/her/my children rise and call him/her/me blessed. _____ is/am stable in all his/her/my ways and not moved by challenges. I declare all financial needs are met and there is no lack. He/she/I will get needed free time and be refreshed to keep on going.

I declare _____ is/am a strong, hardworking, Godly, confident, wise, influential parent!

IT IS SO IN JESUS NAME

Prayer for Teachers

Matthew 10:16 | Titus 2:7 | 1 Corinthians 15:58

Father in the Name of Jesus,

I thank You for _____. Thank You for his/her/their daily sacrifice and that it doesn't go unnoticed. I pray that You would prepare him/her/them each day to welcome the students with a smile and friendly attitude. Let him/her/them set an atmosphere of peace in the classroom and let the classroom be conducive for learning. Let there be peace between _____ and the students and let him/her/them be patient, kind and gentle to every student even in the midst of challenges. Give him/her/ them a passion to teach and to see the students succeed and not work just for a paycheck.

I pray he/she/they will set an example for the students by doing good while teaching with integrity and dignity making a long-lasting positive impact on the life of the students. Give him/her/them funding and resources that are needed so the students will not lack tools that are essential for learning. Bless _____ to continually receive professional development to enhance and improve his/her/their instructional quality. Please help him/her/them to be wise as a serpent, but harmless as a dove, when dealing with difficulties and challenges that arise. Help him/her/them not to label students or prejudge but allow him/her/them to see the root cause of any problems and the wisdom to find solutions.

Build a healthy relationship and trust between _____ and the parents with an open line of communication. Bless him/her/them to know that his/her/their labor, staying late, dealing with challenges, working with difficult students, giving extra help, etc.... is not in vain.

Grace _____ for his/her/their assignment.

IN JESUS NAME, AMEN

Declaration

Father in the Name of Jesus,
Thank You for answering my Prayers!

I declare _____ is a friendly, patient, gentle, kind and amazing teacher. He/she/I will make a positive impact in the lives of many students helping them learn and succeed. I declare _____ is/am passionate, desiring to see all students get a good education and God makes sure all his/her/my needs are supplied and resources available.

I declare _____ will not stop learning and will continually enhance and improve his/her/my teaching. He/she/I know(s) how to handle challenging situations, de-escalate conflict and there is open lines of communication with parents that foster trust and mutual respect.

I declare _____ is/am a smart, strong, wise, compassionate, concerned, trustworthy and loving teacher!

IT IS SO IN JESUS NAME

Prayer for Teenagers

James 1:22 | 1 Timothy 4:12 | Psalm 119:9

Father in the name of Jesus

I pray for _____ to come to the truth, knowledge and confess that Jesus Christ is Lord. Let him/her experience You in such a way that causes him/her to live a life surrendered to You. I pray he/she will not only hear the Word but also will do what the Word says and even though Young he/she will set an example for believers in speech, conduct, love, faith, and purity.

Let him/her learn and believe that his/her identity is found in the Word of God and not in who society says he/she should be. Don't let him/her measure his/her value and worth from how many likes and followers he/she may get on social media but open up his/her understanding to the truth that he/she has been chosen and hand-picked by the king!

Give him/her a boldness to be exactly who You created him/her to be without fear of being judged, talked about, rejected or laughed at. Connect him/her with men and women of God who have integrity, who he/she can be accountable to and honest with when struggling. Don't let him/her mask the pain. Give _____ a mind to say I need help. Disconnect and sever him/her from any friendships, relationships, entanglements and social media connections that were sent by the enemy to derail, distract, lure and pull him/her away from You and the path You have purposed and planned for his/her life. I pray he/she will learn how to handle conflict, disagreements and how to resolve arguments without retaliation. Let him/her be respectful to parents, adults and those in authority.

I pray _____will walk in ordered steps and learn the value of abstinence with a boldness to say no, knowing that he/she can stay on the path of purity by living according to Your word.

IN JESUS NAME, AMEN

Declaration

Father in the Name of Jesus,
Thank You for answering my Prayers!

I declare _____ is a born-again believer who walks in the ways of God, does not straddle the fence and lives a life of holiness.

He/she was born for such a time as this to break stigma's, alter the norm and imitate Christ in this generation! He/she is an example and an influence in speech, conduct, and action, his/her voice is heard and will lead many to Christ.

I declare _____ knows who he/she is and every mask and false identify has been destroyed! His/her friendships are God ordained, selfless and purposeful.

I declare _____ is a bold, uncompromising, focused, respectful, holy child of God!

IT IS SO IN JESUS NAME

Prayer for Thanksgiving

Ephesians 1:4 | 2 Peter 1:3 | John 8:32 | Proverbs 3:12 | Psalm 17:6

Father in the Name of Jesus,

So many times, when we pray we are asking for things, but today I want to stop and take time to say thank You! Lord, I thank You for being good to me. Thank You for life. Thank You that when I was a mess out in the world doing all kinds of wrong, You kept me safe even in my foolishness. Thank You that You chose me even before the world was formed. You looked past all my mistakes and mess ups and seen what I really needed. Thank You that You drew me to You with Your loving kindness. Thank You for a new life in You and sin no longer has power over me. Thank You that I have been empowered with the Holy Spirit to say yes to You and no to my own selfish ways, the ways of the world and to resist the enemy. Thank You that I am an overcomer and through You, I have the victory!

Thank You that You gave me everything I need to live a Godly life. I am without excuse. Thank You for Your Word that instructs me on how to live and to make me aware of Satan's schemes. Thank You that the promises in Your Word apply to me. I can have what Your Word says I can have. Thank You that

I know the truth, and the truth set me free. Thank You that when I do wrong I can confess my sins and You faithfully forgive me and cleanse me from all unrighteousness. Thank You for Your discipline because You love me. Thank You for showing me mercy and holding back what I deserve and showing me grace by giving me what I don't deserve! Thank You that You have plans to prosper me and not harm me, plans to give me hope and a future. Thank You that You are for me. Thank You that I cannot flee from Your presence because You are always with me in good times and bad, and it's not a feeling it's a knowing You are there.

Thank You because I can pray to You the all-knowing, wise and powerful God and I know You hear and will answer me. Thank You for loving me!

IN JESUS NAME, AMEN

Declaration

Father in the Name of Jesus,
Thank You for answering my Prayers!

I will enter His gates with thanksgiving and His courts with praise! I am not ungrateful, but I am thankful and appreciate all God has done and is doing for me and I don't take it for granted but I thank him with a grateful heart.

I will come before him with thanksgiving and extol him with music and song! I thank the Lord for He is good, and His love endures forever, and it is His will I give thanks in all circumstances. I thank the Lord with all my heart and I will tell of His wonderful deeds.

I declare I will devote myself to prayer, being watchful and thankful.

IT IS SO IN JESUS NAME

Prayer for Veterans

Joshua 1:9 | 1 Peter 3:8

Father in the Name of Jesus,

I thank You for the men and women who unselfishly served and serve in our armed forces, who protect and defend our freedom. I pray they forever feel appreciated and loved.

We as civilians don't know what they go through so don't let us forget about them during our daily prayers.

Lord, let those who are still in active duty be strong, courageous, not afraid or discouraged knowing that You Lord are with them even in battle.

Let those who are wounded mentally, emotionally and/or physically receive medical assistance and support to work through the trauma, so they can function successfully. I pray that every need is met during their active time of service as well as when they are no longer on active duty. Help them plan properly to transition back to civilian life and let it be a smooth transition and help them to adjust. Connect them with support groups with like-minded veterans who are sympathetic, loving, compassionate and humble, those they can talk to and don't let them be mistreated, forgotten or feel isolated.

Keep their families intact and safe while they are off selflessly serving in other parts of the world.

Let them receive their full benefits to sustain them after active duty. Remember those who are struggling today to find housing. Connect them with the right person and show them favor so they can get the help they need to get affordable housing. Bless them physically, mentally, emotionally and financially and cause them to thrive in all they do.

IN JESUS NAME, AMEN

Declaration

Father in the Name of Jesus,
Thank You for answering my Prayers!

I declare our veterans are blessed, appreciated, not forgotten and loved! They are healed from all mental and emotional wounds and they have the mind of Christ. They are successfully serving, and their sacrifice does not go unnoticed.

those who are no longer in active duty have adjusted to civilian life and all is well. All financial needs are met, and they are not lacking. Their time and sacrifices are not disregarded but well rewarded.

I declare veterans are selfless, strong, courageous, fearless, encouraged, resilient and blessed.

IT IS SO IN JESUS NAME

Prayer for Wives

Ephesians 5:22 | Proverbs 31:11-12 | Proverbs 27:15 |
Proverbs 14:1

Father in the Name of Jesus,

I thank You that _____ was chosen to be a helpmate and a good thing to her/my husband. I pray that You are first in her/my life. Help her/me be a virtuous woman that her/my husband can trust so she/I will greatly enrich His life and bring him good, not harm all the days of His life. I pray she/I will submit to her/my husband as to the Lord with the right attitude and mindset.

I pray she/I will not be quarrelsome and annoying like a constant dripping on a rainy day but one who controls her/my temper being loving and compassionate with a heart to be more like Christ.

Help her/me to learn what He needs and how to be a support for him and a listening ear. Let her/my words build him up and encourage him and not tear him down and crush His spirit.

Help her/me be a wise woman that builds her house making it a peaceful safe place that her/my husband would desire to come home to and not run from and not a foolish one who tears it down with her own hands. I pray prayer is first on her/my agenda and not last on her/my list. Help her/me be faithful to her/our covenant not letting anyone come between them/us. I pray she/I will be quick to forgive and not easily offended. Help her/me get healed from past hurts and disappointment so fruit from it won't to try negatively impact her/my marriage.

I pray she/I will not compare her/my husband or marriage to someone else, but I will value and appreciate her/my husband and marriage. Help her/me to remember the vows she/I made and have a made-up mind through the good times and bad it's still till death do us part.

(If she has children): help her/me be a Godly mother. Nurturing and loving, patient and wise. Being an example of what a Godly wife and woman of God really lives and looks like. Training and teaching her daughter(s) to love God first and how to pray. To be strong, confident, trustworthy you ladies, who know their value and worth.

IN JESUS NAME, AMEN

Declaration

Father in the Name of Jesus,
Thank You for answering my Prayers!

I declare _____ is/ I am a woman after God's heart and a good thing to her/my husband and He has full confidence in her/me!

She/I walk(s) in power and authority, self-control and wisdom. She's/I'm a righteous woman of God and her/my prayers are powerful and effective! God hears her/me and attends to her/my cry!

She/I will not break her/my covenant, she's/ I'm devoted till the end. She/I speak(s) life over her/my husband and her/my marriage. She/I build(s) her/my husband up and she/I is/am attentive to His needs. _____ is/am loving, patient and kind and has/have His best interest at heart.

I declare _____ is/am a strong, virtuous, faithful, beautiful, holy, bold, powerful wife!

IT IS SO IN JESUS NAME

Prayer for Work Place

Romans 12:11 | 1 Peter 2:13

Father in the Name of Jesus,

With so many out of work and looking for a job, I say thank You Lord for _____ job. Thank You that his/her/my skills and abilities are wanted and needed at _____.

As he/she/I come(s) in each day, I pray for the right attitude and mindset. Let _____ be an example of what a true Christian looks like and acts like.

Let Your Holy Spirit permeate the atmosphere and where there is contention or stress, bring peace, where there is anger or rage bring calmness and patience.

I pray there is teamwork and comradery. Let employees work together and not against each other. Let their/our motives be pure and right. Show them/us how to handle work conflict peacefully and effectively without violence. Fill each meeting with Your peace. Don't let the meetings be stressful, but let all employees see the benefit of meeting and getting the information that they need.

I pray he/she/I will be a good faithful worker. One who is on time, responsible, completes assignments, works hard and is not lazy, but energized, motivated and excited to go to work from day to day. Let him/her/me be a friendly face that awaits coworkers. Give him/her/me wisdom to take a break when needed and not allowing burn out to set in causing frustration and irritation to manifest. Cause him/her/me to submit to those in authority easily and show him/her/me favor in the marketplace.

I pray there be no layoffs and the business will continue to be successful. Let him/her/my pay be fair and appropriate and let all workers feel valued and appreciated. Watch over them/us and keep them/us safe from hurt or harm in the workplace.

IN JESUS NAME, AMEN

Declaration

Father in the Name of Jesus,
Thank You for answering my Prayers!

I declare _____ is an awesome place to work! It's peaceful and the employees are friendly. _____ skills are needed and what he/she/I bring(s) to the table is appreciated.

I declare all employees work together and not against each other. It's team work and unity! _____ can depend on him/her/me and know he/she/I will always do his/her/my best. _____ is/am not lazy or slothful and he/she/I show(s) up on time.

I declare _____ is a successful business. There will not be any layoffs. They pay all workers fair and appropriately.

I declare _____ is/am a faithful, responsible, motivated, dependable hard worker.

IT IS SO IN JESUS NAME

Acknowledgments

Thank You, Jesus! I am so in awe of how You love me. I am so thankful that You listen to my cries and answer my prayers. Your love for me is so soothing. Thank You for choosing me, allowing me and helping me to write this book.

To my husband. My friend. Stevie. Thank You for loving me and believing in me. You are the epitome of a supportive husband. Thank You for allowing me to be me.

A special thank You to my mom Doris Taylor. You have been such a friend. Thank You for always supporting me, believing in me and being there for me.

Meme, oh how I wish You were here to witness the manifested answers to Your prayers. Thank You for training me in the way I should go. I learned about Jesus because of You. And for this, I will be forever grateful.

Ryan Jasmine and Jessica. My loves. Your continual words of encouragement always boost my confidence. I can always depend on You to believe in me. As Your mom, I pray I make You proud to say "she's my mom"

To all the Intercessors who have prayed with me and for me I appreciate You.

Thank You to all those who continually trust me to take Your request to The King.

Love, Hugs, and Prayers!

About the Author

I'm just Your average everyday "girlie girl" who smiled and said everything was fine while struggling secretly with Anorexia, Bulimia, Depression and Suicidal thoughts!

BUT one day I had an encounter with JESUS, my life was forever changed and NOW I'M ON ASSIGNMENT!

Doris D. Harris is the founder of FREE2Bme Ministries. On assignment to help others get free in Jesus! Empowering them to successfully live a life of self-acceptance, self-love, and FREEdom as the beYOUtiful person God created them to be by learning the TRUTH of who they are according to the Word of God, applying the principles found in the Word and developing a steadfast prayer life.

Out of a heart and a passion to serve and help others, Doris D. Harris founded Lending a Helping Hand or 2, Inc. A non-profit personal needs pantry serving those in need in her community. Her goal is to help those in need and in the process put a smile on someone's face.

You can always find her somewhere praying, volunteering or helping someone in need.

About the Publisher

At Vision to Fruition, we are dedicated to helping others bring their personal, business, ministry & nonprofit visions to fruition.

Whether it's as grand as a book You want to write, a business You want to start, a conference or event You want to host, a ministry You want to launch or an organization You want to start; or as small as needing a computer repair, logo design or web design; Vision to Fruition will help You walk through the process and set You up for success! At Vision to Fruition we don't have clients, we have Visionaries. We provide solutions to equip others to pursue their visions & dreams with reckless abandon.

LaKesha is the Lead Visionary behind Overcomers HQ, which is dedicated to helping others overcome, thrive & bring their visions to fruition.

In 2018 we have published twenty-three authors, seven of which were Amazon Bestsellers. We would love for You to join our family of Visionaries as well!!!

Learn more here www.vision-fruition.com

www.ingramcontent.com/pod-product-compliance
Lightning Source LLC
Chambersburg PA
CBHW022157080426
42734CB00006B/476